The Country Houses, Castles and Mansions of Northern Ireland

by Rose Jane Leslie

With photographs from the Des Quail Collection

Antrim Castle

Antrim Castle was built in stages between 1610 and 1666. It was started by Sir Hugh Clotworthy, who had been granted land and the charge of vessels on Lough Neagh by James I, and continued by his son John, a distinguished solder, to whom Charles II awarded the title Baron of Lough Neagh, Viscount of Masserene. In October 1922 Antrim Castle was severely damaged after a fire broke out during a grand ball. One account relates that as soon as the fire was discovered someone was sent to pierce the water tanks at the top of the house but found them empty and the servant responsible for filling them – later said to have IRA sympathies – disappeared. The ruins were demolished in 1970, athough the site, near Antrim town centre, remains as one of only two examples of Dutch-style gardens in Ireland, along with one of the original towers and a castellated gatelodge. In 2008 a Heritage Lottery grant of £3.35m was awarded towards revitalising the gardens. The old stableyard is also still extant and has been developed into an arts centre by Antrim Borough Council.

Text © Rose Jane Leslie, 2011.
First published in the United Kingdom, 2011,
by Stenlake Publishing Ltd.
54-58 Mill Square,
Catrine, KA5 6RD
Telephone: 01290 551122
www.stenlake.co.uk

ISBN 9781840335392

Printed by
P2D Books,
1 Newlands Rd,
Westoning,
Bedford,
MK45 5LD

The publishers regret that they cannot supply copies of any pictures featured in this book.

Acknowledgements

The author wishes to thank Mr and Mrs John Wallace, Mr and Mrs James Leslie, and staff of Belfast Central Library for their assistance in the compilation of material for this book, and also the late Sandy Watson for her help in the early stages of the research. The publishers would like to thank Des Quail for permission to reproduce most of the photographs featured in this book, and also John Wallace for the photograph of Fleming Hall, James Leslie for the photographs of Leslie Hill, Ballyhivistock House, Somerset House and Benvarden House, and Patrick Casement for the photograph of Magherintemple.

Archbishop's Palace, Armagh

In its present form the Archbishop's Palace in Armagh dates from 1825 when Lord John George Beresford, Archbishop of Armagh, added the large entrance porch and an another storey to the original palace which had been built about 1770 for Archbishop Richard Robinson. The demesne contains other interesting features such as a pair of symmetrical linked Georgian houses which were built for the palace farm in the late eighteenth century and the remains of a Franciscan friary which had been founded in 1264. Charles Coote, author of *A Statistical Survey of the County of Armagh* (1804) was apparently impressed by what he saw: 'his grace's farmyard, implements of husbandry and mode of culture afford a bright example to the gentry of what their valuable demesnes could yield under judicious management.' The clergy continued to occupy the palace until 1975, since when it has belonged to Armagh District Council. Today it is used as a municipal office and park, as well as being the headquarters of the North South Ministerial Council and the home of the Armagh Palace Stables Museum.

Introduction

Most of the photographs in this book were published as postcards in the early 1900s; a few date from the 1930s and a small number of images come from private family photograph albums. The houses included here date from the seventeenth century through to the end of the nineteenth century and throughout this period can be traced the rise and fall of country house building in Ulster. The photographs also reflect the range of architectural fashions favoured throughout the centuries and include styles as various as neo-classical, Scottish baronial, Tudorbethan, Gothic and, in one unusual case, neo-Norman.

The history of a large country house or castle is inevitably entwined with that of the family who built it. Most of these families were supported by the income from their estates surrounding the houses and these could amount to many thousands of acres. For the privileged few, ownership of estates became increasingly profitable during the eighteenth century when rents rose, and the period saw the building of great mansions such as Castleward and Baronscourt, as well as other significant houses including Greyabbey, Leslie Hill and Langford Lodge. The Church of Ireland bishops also displayed their wealth in the appearance of bishops' palaces such as those at Armagh and Clogher. Despite their apparent wealth, owners often borrowed large sums to finance the building of these grand houses, accruing debts that often led to financial difficulties for future generations.

Geographically, country houses and castles were concentrated mainly in the counties of Down and Antrim, the most densely populated and economically developed areas of the country, with a few in Co. Armagh and the western counties of Fermanagh, Derry and Tyrone. There is a concentration of houses in Co. Fermanagh around Lough Erne where farmland was rich and examples include Crom Castle and Castle Archdale.

It is sometimes assumed that nearly all landowners acquired their property from lands granted during the time of the plantations in 1610. While some estates, such as Castle Archdale and Castle Irvine, did develop from plantation land grants, or later awards of land, estates could also be extended in a series of private transactions over a period of time, or through marriage to an heiress, or an indirect inheritance which had come about when a family line of male heirs had come to an end. In Ulster, the wealth to support the building of large houses in some cases resulted from the growth of flax and linen manufacture. The linen industry developed in areas such as the Lagan and Bann valleys, introduced there by a number of Quaker families who had moved over from England in the 1600s and who eventually built houses such as Moyallon, Lambeg House and Dunbarton from the profits of their industry. Linen production also took place at Gilford and Lurgan, financing properties such as Gilford Castle, Elmfield and Brownlow House.

In the nineteenth century the taste for neo-classical designs established in the Georgian years persisted until around the 1830s, as shown by examples of houses such as Drenagh and Clandeboye. The period from around 1830 onwards saw the arrival of Victorian castles such as Tandragee and Gosford while other landowners chose to replace their older Georgian houses with Tudorbethan piles like Bangor Castle. Later in the century Scottish baronial was much favoured, examples including Belfast Castle, Stormont Castle and Magherintemple in north Antrim. Most houses were built as a complete entity, while a few evolved throughout several centuries, one example being Red Hall which originated with a seventeenth-century tower house, followed by refurbishments and embellishments in the eighteenth and nineteenth centuries.

The end of the nineteenth century saw the beginning of the gradual decline of country house building and country house life, as landlords faced both increasing economic difficulties and pressure from the tenant rights movement. A solution to the problem was offered in the provisions of the Wyndham Acts of 1903, which enabled landowners to sell to their tenants who were financed by the government. Most landlords then sold the bulk of their estates, giving them a windfall of capital, but leaving them with a large house without enough land to support it. Lack of income gradually led to the disappearance and demolition of some houses as their owners found them too expensive to maintain. The troubles of the 1920s also took their toll, resulting in the burning of Antrim Castle and Crebilly, while Lambeg House perished during the later troubles after 1969. Other families were obliged to hand over their property to the National Trust or sell up entirely. Relatively few such houses are still occupied by the original family who built them, though many remain as family homes.

Ballyards Castle

Situated on the Ballyards Road near Milford, Co. Armagh, and set in 30 acres of parkland, Ballyards Castle was built between 1868 and 1872 by Colonel Thomas Simpson. His forebears first settled in the area around 1713 and became established as producers of linen. Belfast architects Charles Sherry and Robert Hughes were commissioned to design the house, a combination of styles that included Tudor, Venetian and Scottish baronial. After Colonel Simpson died in 1892 the house was bought by Maynard Sinton JP, whose family was also involved in the manufacture of linen with premises in Portadown, Laurelvale and Tandragee. By 1916 various improvements to the house had almost doubled its size. Sinton family members remained at Ballyards Castle until 1962, after which followed spells of use as a private school for boys and a hospital care unit. It changed hands again in 1991 and is now headquarters of the Stauros Foundation and a residential centre for addiction sufferers.

Ballyhivistock

This photograph shows members of the Stuart family, taken at the family home of Ballyhivistock near Derrykeighan, Co. Antrim. The house dates from about 1840 and was built by Charles George Stuart who had been a soldier in the Connaught Rangers from 1811 until his battalion was disbanded after the Battle of Waterloo. Stuart died in 1873 but his widow Maria Christina can be see here, amongst the group on the right, wearing a brimmed black hat and sitting on a garden seat beside one of her sons. The couple had ten children, two of whom – James and Henry – went to Australia in 1874. It is said they left with £50 each in their pockets to seek their fortunes and they had successful careers as sheep farmers. Henry died in Australia in 1902 but James continued, prospered and returned to live in Northern Ireland, settling with his family at Somerset House near Coleraine.

Bangor Castle

Robert E. Ward inherited Bangor Castle in 1837 from his father, Colonel Edward Ward, and rebuilt the Georgian Gothic house in Tudorbethan style, incorporating a music salon that resembles a small church with an organ and stained glass windows commemorating the Ward family. His only daughter, Maude, married Lord Clanmorris from Co. Mayo, thereby passing the property to that family. Lord Clanmorris died in 1916 but his widow lived a further 25 years, retaining the property as her own while her successor, Maurice, lived in South Africa and London in more reduced circumstances. Close family ties remained with Bangor Castle however and the way of life there – a fairly austere regime in which everyone was obliged to eat tiny portions at meal times in deference to the dowager Lady Clanmorris – was vividly recalled in a memoir by Madeleine Bingham who visited there when newly married to John Bingham, the journalist and crime-novelist son of Maurice. In 1941 Bangor Castle was sold to the local authority and now contains the offices of North Down Borough Castle and North Down Museum.

Barons Court

Barons Court, near Newtownstewart, Co. Tyrone, is the seat of the Duke and Duchess of Abercorn and the only ducal residence in Northern Ireland. The first Earl of Abercorn – the dukedom wasn't created until 1868 – settled in the area on land granted in the early seventeenth century; the ruins of the castle he built can still be seen near the present house. The construction of Barons Court was long and complex, starting when George Steuart, a Gaelic-speaking Scottish architect, designed the first version of the house which was completed in 1782. Less than ten years later the first Marquess commissioned significant alterations in which, as proposed by John Soane, the garden front became the entrance front and the portico was moved to its present position. After a fire further alterations by Richard and William Vitruvius Morrison followed between 1836 and 1841. When another fire destroyed the front of the east wing Sir Albert Richardson reduced both wings and the Morrison service wing. More recently, in 1975/76, David Hicks remodelled the interior with characteristic boldness. Barons Court stands in a wooded, landscaped demesne with three lakes, supported by considerable acreage of farmland and commercial forestry.

Belfast Castle

Belfast Castle, designed in Scottish baronial style by Lanyon, Lynn and Co., was completed in 1870 for the third Marquess of Donegall, whose coat of arms is placed above the front door. During the eighteenth century the Donegalls, whose ancestor Sir Arthur Chichester was granted land in Belfast by James I, still owned the city of Belfast, and therefore controlled all building development there although they themselves had lived in England since their original Belfast Castle was burnt down in 1708. In the nineteenth century the Donegalls returned to Belfast, living first at Ormeau Park, but high debts obliged them to sell most of their estates apart from the deer park on Cavehill, where the new castle was built, and the Ormeau demesne, now Ormeau Park. In the grounds of Belfast Castle a Chapel of Resurrection was built as a memorial to Frederick Richard, the only Donegall heir, who died in 1853 at the age of 25. When the remaining daughter, Harriet Chichester, now the heiress, married the Earl of Shaftesbury her property became part of the Shaftesbury estates. They retained the connection with Belfast by using the castle during the summer months, the rest of the time living in England. As figureheads, Lord and Lady Shaftesbury still contributed to local life through activities such as opening the castle grounds for garden fetes and heading the new cathedral subscription list. The nineteenth Earl of Shaftesbury was mayor of Belfast in 1907 and the following year he became the first chancellor of Queen's University. He eventually presented the castle and grounds to Belfast City Council in 1934. The property has since been redeveloped as a hotel and conference centre.

Benvarden House

Benvarden House is just visible in this photograph dating from the 1890s. The house, near Dervock, Co. Antrim, has belonged to the same family since 1798 when Hugh Montgomery, a co-founder of Mongomery's Bank, later the Northern Bank, bought it from the Macnaghten family. Montgomery enlarged the house by adding wings and later an Italianate porch. His son John, a justice of the peace, developed a fearsome reputation and, according to the Rev. Thomas Camac, committed one John Nevin of Ballymoney to Carrickfergus Gaol for shooting a hare on the land at Benvarden. Earlier Nevin had been at the centre of an expensive lawsuit ensuing from his refusal to pay a toll on taking a horse to the Dervock Fair. His defence by Daniel O'Connell, the Irish liberator, resulted in the abolition of tolls. After 1873 Robert Montgomery inherited Benvarden (he was a captain in the 5th Dragoon Guards who served in the Crimean War, seeing action with the Heavy Brigade at the Battle of Balaclava). He added a service wing to the house, removed the glazing bars and built the cast-iron bridge on the left of the photograph which still stands today. In the early 1970s a safari park opened on Benvarden land so that for some 25 years Benvarden was the only Ulster house in which lions could sometimes be heard roaring in the distance.

Carrowdore Castle

Carrowdore Castle at Millisle, Co. Down, was built in 1818 by Nicholas de la Cherois Crommelin, a descendant of Louis Crommelin, who King William III appointed to establish a colony of Huguenot French linen weavers in the Lisburn area at the end of the seventeenth century. This photograph shows the back of the house with the old bawn walls with adjoining summer house flanker and the tall tower leading to a stable yard. In 1902 the contents of the house were sold when the male line of the family came to an end. A number of tenants came and went before Carrowdore Castle was sold in 1962. The house still stands, although the owners have built another on the grounds, and the original gatelodges remain.

Castle Archdale

Castle Archdale, now demolished, stood on the shores of Lower Lough Erne near Lisnarrick, Co. Fermanagh. Built by Colonel Mervyn Archdale in 1778, it was the largest Palladian house in the county. The Archdale family settled in Ulster in the early seventeenth century. John Archdale, a lawyer, was High Sheriff of County Fermanagh in 1616 and an undertaker for lands granted by James I – so called as he had to undertake to build a bawn (fortified house) and keep a company of armed men. According to local tradition, a curse was put on the Archdale family, to the effect that no male heirs would be born within the walls of the bawn, because they took building stones for it from the monastic ruins at Kiltierney nearby. Despite the curse, the family thrived well enough to build the eighteenth-century house seen here and this remained at the heart of a working estate well into the twentieth century. The eventual decline began when Henry Archdale died in 1938 from a heart attack that he suffered on the tennis court of the house. Mervyn Archdale, a cousin from Canada, then inherited, taking up residence and attempting to maintain the property through farming for some years. During the Second World War the property was used as an RAF base. By 1978 the house was derelict and demolished not long after. The gardens and demesne is open to the public as part of Castle Archdale Country Park.

Castle Irvine

Castle Irvine lies near Lower Lough Erne outside Irvinestown, Co. Fermanagh, and is named after Christopher Irvine, a lawyer who leased the land from a Gerard Lowther to whom he was related by marriage sometime in the 1630s. Lowther had taken possession of the land, where a house, bawn and settlement had been established, during the Ulster Plantation of 1610. The house is an amalgamation of the seventeenth-century castle with round towers, to the rear of the current building, with a Tudorbethan façade and extension added to the front during renovations carried out in 1831. The Irvine family remained there until moving to England in 1922. In 1925 Captain Richard Hermon, from Sussex, bought Castle Irvine and lived there with his wife Coralie, née Porter, of Belle Isle, Co. Fermanagh. Captain Hermon died in 1976 and some time later Fermanagh District Council bought the property. Today the house is empty but the land and stables are used as an equestrian centre to host international riding events. It is now known as Necarne Castle, renamed after the ancient Irish placename of *Ni carne e*, meaning 'no stones here'.

Castle Upton

The towers at Castle Upton, Templepatrick, Co. Antrim, no longer have the fairytale conical tops seen in this early 1900s photograph as they were removed later in the twentieth century. The oldest parts of the house, originally fortified, date from the early 1600s, as indicated by a stone marked 1611 in the doorcase at the front of the house. At that time Castle Upton belonged to a Humphrey Norton who leased the property from Sir Arthur Chichester, Lord Deputy of Ireland from 1608, but in 1625 the property was acquired by Sir Henry Upton whose descendants remained there until the deaths of two sons in the First World War. Over the years the house has had various additions, such as interior plasterwork, three large towers, parapets and a stableyard designed by Robert Adam, followed by Edward Blore's neo-Elizabethan windows, internal panelling and the distinctive barbican gatelodge. In the late twentieth century the Kinahan family, by then the owners, undertook to rebuild the ballroom, adding a chimney piece from the Earl Bishop's palace at Downhill.

Castle Ward

In 1570 Bernard Ward settled at Carrick na Sheannagh (which translates as 'the Fox's Rock'), Co. Down, renaming it Castleward and building a fortified tower house. His grandson, the first Viscount Bangor, built Castle Ward in 1762 and the famous dual design of classical on one side (seen here) and Strawberry Hill Gothic on the other was an uneasy compromise between the Viscount and his wife, Lady Anne. Famously, they could not agree on this matter and it is said Lady Anne left the house soon after it was built and spent the rest of her life in Bath. Mrs Delaney visited Castle Ward in 1762 and wrote, 'If they do not do much they cannot spoil the place, for it hath every advantage from nature that can be desired'. In the event the landscaping of the demesne overlooking Strangford Lough was carried out successfully in the style of Capability Brown and was admired by Sir James Caldwell who wrote after visiting in 1772, 'it is, I believe, one of the finest places in this kingdom'. During the nineteenth century the estate flourished but in 1950 was offered in part payment of death duties to the Northern Ireland government and it is now a National Trust property.

Charlemont Fort

Situated in a strategic position on the River Blackwater outside Moy, Co. Tyrone, Charlemont Fort was established at the centre of a military base in 1602 for the lengthy campaign against the O'Neills led by the first Baron Charlemont. In 1641 Phelim O'Neill seized the fort and the third baron, who was living in the garrison with his family, was put to death. This was avenged when the fifth baron captured O'Neill, who was hanged in Dublin in 1653. By 1858 the fort no longer served a military purpose but remained as a landmark to past battles and was sold by the government to Lord Charlemont, who by then lived at Roxborough House across the river. In 1920 it was still regarded as a military threat and was burnt down by Sinn Fein supporters. In a contemporary account, one of the arsonists told the caretaker that the fort was being burnt 'so that no soldiers could be put in it'. Lady Charlemont, by then widowed and living in England, successfully claimed compensation but the ruin was demolished on the advice of the security forces who believed it could be used as a vantage point by snipers.

Clogher Palace

The palace was started in Clogher, Co. Tyrone, in the late eighteenth by Bishop Lord John Beresford, afterwards Archbishop of Armagh, and finished by Bishop Lord Robert Tottenham in 1823. This view is of the garden front; the grounds included a shell grotto, very fashionable in the eighteenth century. In the background stands the tower of St Macartin's Cathedral, named after the first Bishop of Clogher who was appointed in the sixth century. In the late 1800s the house was renamed Clogher Park and became the seat of Thomas Stewart Porter, a descendant of the Right Rev. John Porter, Lord Bishop of Clogher. In latter years Clogher Palace became a convent to the Sisters of St Louis and is now used as a residential nursing home.

Craigavad House

Craigavad House in Co. Down was built on the shores of Belfast Lough in 1852 for John Mulholland, later the first Lord Dunleath. Mulholland lived there until he inherited Ballywalter Park after his father Andrew died in 1866. The Mulhollands introduced the flax spinning industry to Belfast and opened the highly successful York Street spinning mill in 1830. A house seems to have been existence on the site since the late eighteenth century when Mrs Pottinger, a member of a family of merchant ship owners, lived there. After John Mulholland moved out Craigavad House was let to a succession of tenants before the freehold was sold to Sir Robert Kennedy, who later built Cultra Manor, but then changed hands several times until Lady Edith White sold it to the Royal Belfast Golf Club in 1925.

Crebilly House

Situated outside Ballymena, between Kells and Broughshane, Crebilly originally belonged to the O'Hara family who came to the townland of Ballyclug around 1350 during the reign of Henry II. By the mid-nineteenth century the Italianate mansion in the photograph had been built by Henry O'Hara, a character with a certain reputation for wildness whose wife, it is said, decided to leave him after he poured hot coals in her lap when she refused to greet him and his friends returning home after a drunken evening. He died in 1875 and is probably the inspiration for a local ghost story which relates that on Christmas Eve a figure on a white mare can be seen galloping from the graveyard where O'Hara is buried to jump a gate before disappearing from a bridge into the water below. The last O'Hara to live at Crebilly was Mrs Wardlaw, née O'Hara, who died around 1888 after which it passed to the Dinsmore family of Ballymoney. The IRA burnt the house down in 1922 on the night of a formal ball and all that now remains is the stable yard and gatelodge.

Crom Castle

Crom Castle, near Newtownbutler, Co. Fermanagh, stands on high ground above an inlet of Upper Lough Erne. Designed by Edward Blore, an English architect specialising in the Gothic Revival style, the house was constructed from 1834 for the third Earl of Erne, John Crichton. Blore also designed the farmyard and boathouse, and oversaw the creation of a picturesque demesne that includes follies such as an island tower house and the preserved ruins of an earlier Crom Castle dating from the 1610 plantation. The Crichton family settled there after Abraham Crichton, MP for Augher, bought the property from his father in law, James Spottiswoode, Bishop of Clogher, in 1695. In the nineteenth century agriculture at the Crom estate developed and still thrived in the 1930s, the time of this photograph, employing at least 40 people. In 1940 the fifth earl was killed in the war, leaving a young family including Henry, the present Earl of Erne, who was aged two at the time of his father's death. He came of age in 1958 and still lives at the castle. The estate of over 1,300 acres is in the care of the National Trust while Crom Castle remains the family's private residence with the west wing let as short-term holiday accommodation.

Cultra Manor

Sir Robert Kennedy built Cultra Manor, in Craigavad, Co. Down, during the late nineteenth century to replace an earlier house; his ancestor, John Kennedy, had bought the estate of Cultra from the Earl of Clanbrassil in 1671. Sir Robert Kennedy was a distinguished diplomat whose career as an attaché took him to locations as varied as Madrid, Constantinople, St Petersburg, Bulgaria, Romania, Uruguay and Montenegro. In 1880 he married Bertha Ward, a daughter of the fifth Viscount Bangor of Castle Ward. Family history relates that when Sir Robert asked Bertha's father for her hand in marriage, he also offered a stuffed bear that he had shot in Russia. The bear was duly accepted and is still at Castle Ward. Sir Robert died in 1936, leaving three daughters, one of whom, Matilda Kathleen, was still living in Craigavad at the family seat referred to in the 1958 edition of *Burke's Landed Gentry* as Kennedy Lodge, also on the Cultra Estate and possibly a different name for Cultra Manor. Since the early 1960s the property and land has belonged to the Ulster Folk and Transport Museum.

Derrymore House

It is said that the Act of Union of 1801 was drafted in the drawing room of Derrymore House, the home of Isaac Corry, MP for Newry and the last Chancellor of the Irish Exchequer, whose friend Lord Castlereagh was closely involved in the negotiations. Situated near Bessbrook, Co. Armagh, the house was built around 1776 and is an example of the cottage ornee, a type of house fashionable for a while amongst romantically minded members of the gentry. Despite having only a single storey and a thatched roof, Derrymore has the hallmarks of a gentleman's residence with a number of sitting rooms, bedrooms, landscaped grounds and two gatelodges. Isaac Corry (1755–1813) came from the landed family of Corry from Rockcorry, Co. Monaghan. He studied law and was called to the Irish Bar in 1779, but soon after became involved with politics. He never married but is thought to have had six illegitimate children. The property was sold in 1810 and later went to the Richardson family who had built the model village of Bessbrook. In 1952 John S.W. Richardson gave the house and its 48-acre grounds to the National Trust.

Drenagh

This view of Drenagh, near Limavady in Co. Derry, shows a balustrade behind which lies Italian-style terraced gardens and a fountain inspired by the Villa d'Este near Rome. There is also a distinctive Chinese garden with a circular 'Moon Gate', designed in the 1960s by Lady Margaret McCausland. Drenagh, which was built around 1837, is one of the first important country houses to be designed by Charles Lanyon. It was commissioned by Marcus McCausland to replace an eighteenth century house known as Fruit Hill, which stood on a site nearby. The first of the McCauslands to settle on the property, Colonel Robert McCausland, was the great grandson of Baron Alexander McAuslane, a member of the Scottish house of McAuslane of Buchanan, who came to Ireland in the 1540s. Colonel McCausland had succeeded to estate under the will of the Right Honourable William Conolly, Speaker of the Irish House of Commons. Drenagh is still owned by the McCausland family.

Drum Manor

Drum Manor near Cookstown, Co. Tyrone, was originally built in the eighteenth century by the Richardson family but rebuilt in 1829 by Major Richardson Brady to include big gables and battlemented bay windows. After he died the property passed down the female line until, in 1866, Augusta Vicomte, the only surviving child of Major William Stewart Richardson Brady, married Lord Castlestewart whose own family seat was situated not far from Cookstown at Newtownstewart. At this stage the large Gothic porch and tower, designed by William Hastings of Belfast, were added. The coat of arms at each entrance may reflect the amalgamation of both families as Augusta Vicomte, being the last in her family line, assumed the Richardson Brady name and coat of arms in her own right, while Lord Castlestewart took the surname of Richardson and Stewart. In 1964 Drum Manor was taken over by the Forestry Service and in 1975 the house was partially demolished, leaving only the outside shell. A garden created within the ruins is still maintained and the property is open to the public, managed by the Department of Agriculture for Northern Ireland.

Drumbanagher

Designed by Playfair, the celebrated Edinburgh architect, the construction of Drumbanagher, an enormous Italianate mansion near Poyntzpass, started around 1837 for Colonel Maxwell Close and his wife Anna, née Brownlow of Brownlow House, Lurgan. Playfair insisted on using only materials of the highest quality and also designed the furniture, recommended wallpaper (flock for the dining room), and initiated the purchase of books for the library. Correspondence of the time shows that any cost-cutting measures suggested by Colonel and Mrs Maxwell-Close were dismissed and a total of £80,000 was spent on the house and the outbuildings. Drumbanagher was recognised as one of Playfair's grandest private houses and the working drawings are preserved in Edinburgh University Library. Despite its architectural significance the original owner's descendants demolished Drumbanagher in 1962 because of maintenance costs, death duties and other financial difficulties. All that remains of the house is the vast entrance porch.

Dunbarton House

During the First World War Dunbarton House at Gilford, Co. Down, was a convalescent home run by the Ulster Volunteer Force Nursing Corps. It is also one of very few houses in Northern Ireland to have its own Second World War air-raid shelter, built by American soldiers stationed there at the time, along with a squash court and swimming pool. The house dates from 1845, built for Hugh Dunbar of the Dunbar McMaster mill in Gilford, and the design is attributed to the architect Thomas Jackson. At the time Gilford Mill was one of the largest in Ireland, drawing employees from the counties of Monaghan, Fermanagh and Armagh. To accommodate them, Hugh Dunbar built 180 houses, granted land and contributions towards Methodist, Presbyterian, Roman Catholic churches, and set aside houses for a fever hospital. He died intestate in 1847 and the estate and mills passed to his sisters who were eventually bought out by John Walsh McMaster in 1859. Gilford Mill operated until the late 1980s and today the house is privately owned.

Elmfield Castle

The Scottish baronial-style Elmfield Castle was built for James Dickson, a partner in the Dunbar, Dickson and Co. linen thread company in Gilford. Situated to the northwest of Gilford, the house was built after Dickson bought the land in 1861 from the Christy family. He commissioned William Spence, the same Scottish architect who designed Gilford Castle for his brother Benjamin, to design the house but then sold Elmfield in the 1870s. In 1884 Mr Foster Green, a Belfast tea and coffee merchant, bought the house for his daughter Emily on her marriage to Henry Albert Uprichard, whose family owned the Springvale Bleachworks at Lawrencetown, Co. Armagh. For nearly 70 years Elmfield was the main Uprichard residence. The family were enthusiastic equestrians and built up extensive stables there. William Foster Uprichard was a successful amateur jockey who became Irish Amateur Champion, as did his son, Richard Rutledge Kane Uprichard (known as 'Rut'). Elmfield was inherited by Rut in 1949 but he died in 1952, leaving no heir, and the property was sold to the Shaw family who remain there today.

Fleming Hall

In 1747 Christopher Fleming secured a lease from Lord Antrim for lands at Anticur near Dunloy, Co. Antrim, where Fleming Hall, an early Georgian house is situated. He was a great nephew of Colonel Christopher Fleming, 22nd Baron Slane, who was given a home and refuge in the same area by his kinsman Lord Antrim, to whom the land belonged at the time. Colonel Fleming had fought on the losing side, the Jacobites, at the battles of the Boyne and Aughrim for which he endured imprisonment, forfeit of his peerage, and exile. Christopher Fleming died in 1771 and eventually the property passed to Sarah Fleming, who married James Leslie, the builder of Leslie Hill, Ballymoney, in 1789. Sarah was James Leslie's second wife, some 20 years younger than he. According to local stories, Sarah brought her own horse with her to Leslie Hill and the animal lived to be over 50 years old, well beyond its natural lifespan. Some years later Fleming Hall was sold to Mr Richards and in 1836 to the Wallace family to whom it still belongs.

Gilford Castle

Benjamin Dickson, a partner in the Dunbar McMaster linen thread company which was based in Gilford, Co. Down, built the present Gilford Castle after he bought the land in 1855. Close by there stood a castle, by then abandoned, belonging to the Johnston family who had earlier connections with Gill Hall and owned estates at Gilford. It had been empty since 1841 when Sir William Johnston had died unmarried. His sisters, Catherine and Mary Anne, both inherited and Catherine sold her part to Benjamin Dickson. The old castle was later demolished and William Spence, a Scottish architect, was employed to design the present Scottish baronial Gilford Castle, built in Portland stone and Scrabo standstone. The property passed to trustees when Benjamin Dickson died in 1894 and was bought by James Wright in 1918. His family still own the castle today.

Gill Hall

Captain John Magill built Gill Hall near Dromore, Co. Down, around 1670–80. By 1765 it had passed through the marriage of the last surviving child of the family, Theodosia Magill, to the Earls of Clanwilliam. The house developed a reputation for being the most haunted in Ireland due to the strange story of Lady Beresford who, on a visit to Gill Hall in October 1693, saw an apparition of her cousin, the Earl of Tyrone, who had died the previous week. The apparition told her that she would die on her 47th birthday and seized her wrist, leaving burn marks on the skin. Lady Beresford did indeed die on her 47th birthday, and the story goes that her ghost haunted a bedroom in Gill Hall. For a while those seeking a sight of the ghost, always elusive, were charged sixpence to see the chamber where it supposedly resided. In 1910 the fifth Earl of Clanwilliam moved to nearby Montalto with his new bride who refused to live there any longer, claiming that the presence of ghosts made the house unbearable to remain in. Left empty for many years, the Irish Georgian Society made repairs to the house in 1966. Restoration work was never completed however, and Gill Hall was finally demolished in the early 1990s.

Glynn Park House

A reference in the Ordnance Survey memoirs indicates that Glynn Park House in Carrickfergus, Co. Antrim, dates from the late eighteenth century and was built by James Craig Esq.; however, it was the residence of John Legg Esq. when the memoirs were published in the 1830s. It was described then as a 'small but neat looking edifice', but judging from this view it must have been enlarged at a later date. This photograph was used as a postcard and a handwritten note on the back stating 'the Mayor's House' refers to Frederick Coates – stockbroker and insurance agent, Justice of the Peace, Mayor of Belfast, and High Sheriff for Belfast in 1906 – who lived there. The car parked at the front of the house probably belonged to Coates who was, according to Robert M. Young's *Belfast and the Province of Ulster* (1902), a motoring enthusiast and one of the first people in Northern Ireland to own a car. In its heyday the entrance of Glynn Park would have been recognised easily by the stone sphinxes on the pillars of the front gates. Unfortunately, these no longer exist and a road separates the gate lodge from the house, which is now on Taylor's Avenue and surrounded by development.

Gosford Castle

Gosford Castle near Markethill, Co. Armagh, was designed by the leading London architect Edward Hopper for Archibald Acheson, the second Earl of Gosford, and took over 30 years to build, starting in 1819 and completed about 1850. The Acheson family had lived in the Markethill area since the seventeenth century when Sir Archibald Acheson was granted land in the counties of Armagh and Cavan. The Neo-Norman style of Gosford Castle did not turn out to be popular; the only other British example is Penrhyn Castle in Wales, perhaps because the interiors tended to be dark and cramped. Instead the Scottish baronial style, favoured by Queen Victoria, became fashionable. The Acheson family moved out of Gosford Castle in 1921 and sold it after the Second World War, during which it had been requisitioned by British and US soldiers. It was then used as a store for the Public Records Office and later by the British Army during the Northern Ireland troubles. In 1978 a lease was granted to a consortium of businessmen who opened it as a restaurant and nightclub for a short time. In 2006 Gosford Castle was sold by the Department of Agriculture and Rural Development for renovation and conversion into 23 residential apartments.

Greyabbey House

William Montgomery, whose ancestor Sir Hugh Montgomery had moved to Co. Down from lowland Scotland in the early seventeenth century, built Greyabbey House around 1762. There is documentary evidence of an earlier house on the same site from 1683, when the owner William Montgomery referred to a 'double roofed house' called Rosemount, a name that was still used for the house instead of Greyabbey in the early twentieth century. The house overlooks Strangford Lough and this photograph shows the entrance front, with the door at the side. On the garden front there are three gothic windows, which as suggested by Mark Bence Jones, could have been added later as a result of the influence of the Gothic-design part of Castle Ward, also overlooking Strangford Lough, particularly as William Montgomery's son, the Rev. Hugh Montgomery, married the Hon. Emilia Ward, a daughter of the first Viscount Bangor in 1782. In the grounds are the ruins of a Cistercian monastery from which both the house and the nearby village of Greyabbey takes their name. This was founded in 1193 by Afric, wife of John de Courcy, for monks brought over from the Abbey of Holme-Cultarnin in Cumberland.

Groomsport House

Built of cream sandstone imported from Glasgow, Groomsport House dates from about 1850. It was designed for John Waring Maxwell of Finnebrogue, Downpatrick. In the nineteenth century the Maxwell family owned the small fishing village of Groomsport near Bangor, Co. Down, where the house stands close to the seashore. The Jacobethan design has been attributed to the English architect James Sands, who also worked on Hillsborough Castle. For a while Groomsport House was a hotel, but it has since been converted into apartments and new houses have been built close to the house, crowding out the approach and the clear sweeping views of Cove Bay that the owners would have enjoyed when this photograph was taken.

Killyleagh Castle

The Norman Knight John de Courcy first built fortifications in defence against Vikings on the site of Killyleagh Castle, Co. Down, in the late twelfth century. The castle originates with the Hamilton family, who settled at Killyleagh in 1625 and whose descendants are still *in situ*. The seventeenth-century castle was partly destroyed by Cromwellian forces in 1649, but was rebuilt in 1665 by Henry Hamilton, the second Earl of Clanbrassil, who also restored the bawn walls. In the mid-nineteenth century the castle was enlarged to the designs of Charles Lanyon, who added the romantic towers and turrets seen on the house today. For almost 200 years of its history Killyleagh Castle was divided between two families of Hamilton descendants, one occupying the main house while the other lived in the bawn and gate house, the result of a legal wrangle over inheritance between cousins after the second Earl died without issue in 1667. The feud was finally resolved in 1847 when the then owner of the gatehouse, Lord Dufferin (later the first Marquess of Dufferin and Clandeboye), gave it to the Hamiltons in the main house in return for a rent of a golden rose and a pair of golden spurs to be presented on alternate years, a chivalrous practice that no longer continues although a silver rose and spurs are still preserved at the Dufferin family seat, Clandeboye House.

Lambeg House

Lambeg House, built by Alexander Williamson around 1785, was one of several houses linked to families prominent in the linen industry of the Lagan Valley, southwest of Belfast. The house remained in the Williamson family until 1849 when it passed to John Richardson, owner of another firm of linen bleachers whose descendants went on to live there for over 100 years. During its history the property was first known as Lambeg Village House, then changed when another Lambeg House nearby was renamed Glenmore. The photograph shows a chain fence along the edge of the lawn, causing it to be known colloquially as 'The Chains' during the 1930s. At that time the Misses Bertha and Norah Richardson, the last of the family to live there, were in residence. After Norah Richardson died in 1942 the house passed through several owners before becoming a hotel, which was destroyed by a terrorist bomb in 1975.

Langford Lodge

Langford Lodge, a Georgian mansion on the Lough Neagh shore near Crumlin, Co. Antrim, was built on lands awarded to Sir Roger Langford for service to the crown in the early seventeenth century, later passing to the Pakenham family, the Earls of Longford, through marriage in 1796. Subsequent occupants included Sir Hercules Pakenham, a Peninsular War general whose sister, Kitty, married the Duke of Wellington. Another descendant, Colonel H.A. Pakenham, a Grenadier Guard, was in the Northern Ireland senate. In February 1929 the *Lisburn Herald* described him as 'the fastest speaker in the Senate…an exception to the rule that soldiers do not excel at public speaking'. In 1940 Langford Lodge was sold to the Air Ministry and Glenn Miller entertained American service personnel there during the Second World War. In 1959 the property was sold to MB Aircraft Ltd, a leading manufacturer of ejector seat technology. The house was demolished and the site is now an industrial complex. The airfield is still in evidence and home to two model flying clubs although, memorably, a Dan Air BAe 748 en route to nearby Belfast International Airport landed there by mistake on 2 March 1989.

Leslie Hill

Leslie Hill, outside Ballymoney, Co. Antrim, was built in 1755 for James Leslie, second son of Peter Leslie, Rector of Ahoghill. In the seventeenth century James's ancestor William Leslie (younger son of the Most Rev. Henry Leslie, Bishop of Down and Meath) settled in the nearby townland of Cloughcorr about a quarter of a mile from the present house, having bought the property from the Hamilton family in 1674. Mrs Delany, an artist and writer, went to Leslie Hill in 1758 and found the house 'unfinished and full of company but they crammed us in, and it was better than any inn we could go to'. This carefully arranged photograph of a Leslie family group includes Colonel Edmund Douglas Leslie, who succeeded to the property in 1880, and probably two of his sisters, showing an evident interest in archery, which in the 1870s had become the first competitive sport open to women. The colonel died unmarried in 1903. He was succeeded by his nephew, James Graham Leslie, Privy Councillor, His Majesty's Lieutenant for Co. Antrim, barrister, and senator in the Northern Ireland Parliament at Stormont between 1921 and 1949. His descendants still live in the house today.

Loughbrickland House

The Whyte family of Loughbrickland House in Co. Down have a lineage that can be traced back to 1170 when Sir Walter Whyte accompanied Richard de Clare, known as Strongbow, on his expedition to Ireland. Whyte's descendant, Nicholas Charles Whyte, Deputy Lieutenant of the County, Justice of the Peace and High Sheriff, built the house in 1830. John Whyte DL was the owner in 1875 when the house was described in Knox's *History of County Down* as 'one of the principle gentleman's seats in the Parish of Aghaderg'. The golden wedding anniversary celebration of Mr Whyte and his wife in 1912 was recorded in the *Household Almanac* of 1913 and featured entertainment for many of the people of the district. Children at local schools were given a holiday and taken to a matinee in the Banbridge Picture House, while a barn dance was held that evening. The Whytes received an array of presents such as a golden bowl, vases, photo frames and goblets. Among the congratulatory telegrams to arrive was a message of blessing from the Pope through Cardinal Merry de Val. Loughbrickland House still belongs to the Whyte family.

Loughgall Manor

Loughgall Manor lies in the village of Loughgall, in the midst of Co. Armagh's apple growing area. Dating from about 1840, the house was built by the Cope family. Sir Anthony Cope of Hanwell, Oxfordshire, settled in Co. Armagh, having bought the manors of Loughall and neighbouring Carrowbrack from Lord Saye and Sele who had been granted property in the plantations of the previous year. In 1643 the manor was sacked and burnt down after a battle between Scottish and Irish armies, an incident that led from the rebellions of 1641 when the Irish attacked many of the Plantation settlements. Thereafter came more settled circumstances in which the Cope family developed their estates on which apple orchards were cultivated. Loughgall village also developed under the Cope family's influence; a school was built and money bequeathed for a church. In the early 1900s there were no public houses at Loughgall, as the Cope family had bought them and closed them down, and there are still none today.

Magherintemple

Magherintemple stands above the Co. Antrim coastal town of Ballycastle. The dominant main block of the house with its Scottish baronial crowsteps, was built around 1875 to adjoin the ivy covered two-storey part, which dates from the mid eighteenth century. The figure on the steps in the photograph is probably John Casement JP, who built the house and who was High Sheriff in 1881. The old house was originally known as Churchfield and was leased by the Stewarts of Ballintoy to Hugh Harrison, son of the Rev. Michael Harrison, Vicar of Culfeightrim and Ramoan. Hugh married Mary Casement and when he died in 1786 Mary, left with ten children, sold the property to her brother Roger Casement, a solicitor then living in Ballymena. The Casement family still own the property today.

Montalto House

When this photograph was taken in the early 1900s Montalto House at Ballynahinch, Co. Down, was the property of the Ker family who bought it from the Earls of Moira in 1802. Originally Montalto was a two-storey Georgian house but a third storey was added in 1837 by the adventurous method of digging out the bedrock underneath the house and round its foundations, then lowering the surrounding ground to bring it to the correct level, while many pillars and arches were added to support the structure. A ballroom and service wing were built but these were demolished in 1952. The Kers did not live permanently at Montalto until after 1844 when their other house at Portavo, near Donaghadee, burnt down. The family settled in Northern Ireland when David Ker, who had successfully developed a linen business in London, bought Portavo in 1765, initially as an investment. In 1912 Montalto was sold to the Earl of Clanwilliam, whose wife it is said refused to live at Gill Hall, Dromore, because it was haunted. The Kers returned to Portavo and Montalto is still in private hands although it was sold by the Earl of Clanwilliam around 30 years ago.

Mount Stewart

The two girls in this photograph are Ladies Helen and Margaret Vane Tempest Stewart, daughters of the seventh Marquess of Londonderry. It was taken in the early 1920s when they were aged about 12 and 13, in the gardens behind Mount Stewart House, Newtownards, Co. Down, where their ancestor Alexander Stewart bought property in 1744. Lady Margaret later married Alan Muntz, a German businessman who was involved in setting up Gatwick Airport. They met when Alan Muntz had visited her parents at Mount Stewart. Lord Londonderry was Air Minister between 1931 and 1935 and was finally excluded from politics when he became a proponent of negotiations with Nazi Germany as a means of avoiding the outbreak of the Second World War. He died in 1949. At the height of their influence the Londonderrys owned collieries in the North of England, five country houses, and Londonderry House in London. Mount Stewart has been in the care of the National Trust since 1976. Lady Mairi Bury, the youngest daughter, spent most of her life there, establishing on the estate the first thoroughbred stud in Northern Ireland. She died in November 2009.

Moyallon House

Thomas Christy Wakefield built Moyallon House, near Gilford, Co. Down, in 1794. His ancestor, Alexander Christy, had settled in Moyallon townland around 1710 and the Christy family is regarded as having introduced linen manufacture to Bann Valley; Thomas Christy Wakefield's father, Joseph Wakefield, owned Moyallon bleach green in the late eighteenth century. Both families were Quakers, forming part of a closely related group that was involved with linen manufacture in the area. In the late nineteenth century Moyallon had become the property of the Richardson family, who were also linked to the linen industry, following the marriage of John Grubb Richardson to Jane Marion Wakefield. The Richardson family remain owners of the house today.

Old Court

In celebration of his marriage in 1853, Dudley Charles Fitzgerald de Ros was given a lime tree-lined avenue to his house, Old Court, by Frederick Hamilton Templeton Blackwood, first Marquess of Dufferin and Ava. Lord de Ros was equerry to HRH the Prince Consort between 1853 and 1861, then Lord in Waiting to Queen Victoria from 1874 to 1880. Old Court, shown here, was built near the entrance to Strangford Harbour, Co. Down, in 1844 and was burnt down in 1920 during troubles caused by the Civil War. A smaller house was then built on the same site. The title of de Ros is of ancient Scottish origin, and a Robert de Ros is recorded as leader of the 25 Barons appointed to enforce the Magna Carta. A little church dating from 1629 lies in the grounds; this was built by one Valentine Pain, an agent of the Earl of Kildare who owned the town of Strangford at the time, having been granted it by Henry VIII. Today the church is used as a chapel of ease for the parish.

Portglenone House

Although the property of the Alexander family, Portglenone House, Co. Antrim, was for a time the residence of Miss Anne Young ('Annie'), a relation of the Young family of Galgorm Castle near Ballymena. In her recollections, Mary Alice Young wrote that Annie went to Portglenone House 'at the end of a romance with the old Alexander bachelors. Instead of leaving the place to their next of kin, who fully expected it, they left it to her and they used to have shooting parties. One day that year [in 1907] we got 23 pheasants and 13 woodcock. She always gave an excellent lunch and everyone enjoyed going there.' Nathaniel Alexander, Bishop of Down and Connor, later Bishop of Meath and nephew of the first Lord Caledon, built Portglenone House around 1810, having demolished the old castle in the grounds. The columns of the porche cochere are pink marble, brought back from Rome by Frederick Hervey, the Bishop of Derry (known as the Earl-Bishop). Miss Young died at Portglenone in 1921 and the property then returned to the rightful heir, Arthur Alexander. In 1948 Portglenone House was sold by Major R.C. Alexander and is now a Cistercian Monastery, Our Lady of Bethlehem Abbey, with a community of some 20 monks at the time of writing.

Red Hall

Red Hall, near Ballycarry, Co. Antrim, was built around a seventeenth-century tower house, on lands leased to a William Edmonstone from Scotland whose family remained there until Richard Ker, of the Montalto family, bought Red Hall in 1780. The transaction was not straightforward, however, as old Mrs Edmondstone, aged over 83, was still living there and would not be moved. Richard Ker was obliged to set up home in a Ballycarry inn, bringing servants, beds and everything from Portavo, the other family seat, planning to live there until the old lady died which did not happen until 1784. On eventually settling there, he built the wings shown here and possibly also the front doorcase. The building history of the house is complicated: the square turret is a later Victorian addition, as were the plate glass windows, while inside the house there is early eighteenth-century plasterwork and an early seventeenth-century staircase. The Ker family sold Redhall in 1868 after which it changed hands several times, with most of the land sold off, before Vice-Admiral McClintock bought it in 1927. Today, the house remains in the McClintock family.

Richhill Castle

Richhill Castle, in the village of Richhill, Co. Armagh, was built around 1665 by Major Edward Richardson, MP for Armagh, to replace an earlier manor house belonging to the family of his wife, Anne Sacheverall, whose father was granted the land in 1618. The distinctive Dutch gables are characteristically of the seventeenth-century English style; in Northern Ireland the only other house to have this feature was Echlinville in Co. Down before it was rebuilt in the nineteenth century. Richill is also regarded as one of the earliest large country houses to have been built without defensive features in the years after the restoration of Charles II. The house remained in the Richardson family until the end of the nineteenth century. Samuel Lewis noted their benevolence as proprietors of Richhill village in his *Topographical Dictionary of Ireland* (1837), writing that 'the poor of the neighbourhood of Richhill benefit from the munificence and philanthropy of the Hon. Mrs Caulfield and the Misses Richardson'. Richhill Castle is still in private ownership, but in urgent need of repair and was added to the World Monuments Watch List of the 100 most endangered sites of 2008.

Roe Park

Situated on the banks of the River Roe outside Limavady, Co. Derry, Roe Park developed over the years into the very long house that it is today. It was originally built in the eighteenth century as a seven-bay two-storey house by the Right Hon. William Conolly (1662–1729), Speaker of the Irish House of Commons. Conolly, originally from Co. Donegal, was a successful lawyer and is thought to have become the richest man in Ireland of his time, having made money through property transactions dealing in forfeited estates after the Battle of the Boyne in 1690. He built the renowned Castletown House in Co. Kildare. Roe Park passed to Marcus McCausland in 1743, after which the house – by that time called Mullagh – was renamed as Daisy Hill and enlarged with a dining room. It passed next to John Cromie and was then bought by Sir Francis Macnaghten in 1826, who added a drawing room and renamed it Roe Park. By 1886 the house belonged to a Mrs E.J.S. Ritter who had succeeded to the property after her uncle, Samuel Maxwell Alexander. Today, the house is in commercial use as the Roe Valley Hotel and Country Park.

Scarva House

Distinctive for the Jacobean-style features on its exterior, additions that were carried out from between 1833 and 1861, Scarva House in Co. Down was originally built around 1717 by Miles Reilly. The Reilly family descended from the Princes of East Breffny, an old Irish family who owned extensive estates around Banbridge. The demesne is noted for having a 'venerable' oak tree under which William of Orange is said to have pitched his tent on the way to the Battle of the Boyne. Today a commemorative 'sham fight' re-enactment of the Williamite battles of the Boyne, Aughrim, Derry and Enniskillen takes place on July 13 every year in the grounds of the house, carried out by the Schomberg Society. Another site of antiquarian interest nearby is the remains of the Danes Cast or the Glen of the Black Pig, an ancient trench dug for defensive purposes. Excavations of the trench during the construction of the Newry Canal in 1807 resulted in finds of arrowheads, spearheads, a gold tiara, swords and the vast antlers of an Irish elk.

Somerset House

Somerset House, near the River Bann outside Coleraine, Co. Derry, was built in the nineteenth century for the Richardson family. Bence Jones describes it as a 'nineteenth century villa deriving from the villas of Richard Morrison' and in Morrison's own words the villa design was intended to provide 'a residence that should combine simplicity and purpose of a large family, or of affluent fortune, while it retained the modest character of becoming the habitation of an unostentatious private gentlemen'. By the late 1800s the house had passed through marriage to the Torrens family but some time after 1912 was bought by James Stuart, originally from Ballyhivistock, who settled there with his family having returned home from a life of sheep farming in Australia. The Stuarts remained there for some 40 years but since then the house has disappeared, submerged by the growth of the Monsanto industrial plant and retail developments on the outskirts of Coleraine.

Stormont Castle

Since 2007 Stormont Castle has been the headquarters of the office of the First Minister and the Deputy First Minister, and also the main meeting place of the Northern Ireland Executive. In its present form the house dates from 1858 when the Belfast architect Thomas Turner was commissioned by the Cleland family to extend the previous house on the site, which, as recorded in the 1837 Ordnance Survey memoirs, was the residence of Samuel Cleland Esq. – 'a large plain house with very little planting about it'. The old house was built by the Rev. John Cleland, Rector of Newtownards, tutor to the young Lord Castlereagh, who in his career as Foreign Secretary brought about the Congress of Vienna at the end of the Napoleonic Wars in 1815. The Cleland family left Stormont Castle in 1893 and for a period it was let to Charles E. Allen JP, a director of the Belfast shipbuilding firm, Workman and Clark. In 1921 the house, having failed to reach a good price at auction, was acquired as a site for the administrative buildings of the new Northern Ireland government, created as a result of the partition of Ireland in 1921. From then until 1972 Stormont Castle was designated the official residence of the Prime Minister of Northern Ireland although in practice the only Prime Minister to live there was James Craig (Lord Craigavon) until 1940. Otherwise, from 1921 until 1972, Stormont Castle contained the Cabinet Room of the government and was used by MI5 officers during the Troubles. Before devolution it was also the headquarters of the Secretary of State for Northern Ireland and ministers of the Northern Ireland Office.

Stranocum House

Stranocum House, which lies about five miles from Ballymoney, Co. Antrim, dates from the later eighteenth century, when the land was held by the Hamilton family, who were connected with Leslie Hill at Ballymoney. By the early 1800s the house was the property of the Hutchinson family. George Hutchinson, a magistrate, was responsible for the sentencing of several rebels involved in the 1798 rebellion in Ballymoney, some of whom, notoriously, were hanged in the town. In 1856 Stranocum House passed to William Higginson Ford, a relation, who afterwards assumed the name of Ford Hutchinson on succession to the property. Valuations of rateable property in Ireland in 1861 and 1876 show that William F. Hutchinson owned land extending to 2,370 acres around Stranocum as well as the village itself, houses and offices, a saw mill and school. His descendant, the Rev. William Ford Hutchinson went to New Zealand in 1912, around which time the house was let to James Stuart, whose family members are recognisable in the photograph, before they moved to Somerset House near Coleraine. The Hutchinson family left Stranocum House in the 1950s, although it is still in private hands and has since been fully restored.

Tandragee Castle

For many years Tandragee Castle was the inspiration for the cartoon castle image on Tayto crisp packets. The real Tandragee Castle, in Co. Armagh, is used as offices for the Tayto crisp factory, which is based in the grounds, and is run by the Hutchinson family who established the company after buying the property in 1955. George Montagu, sixth Duke of Manchester, built the castle in 1837 on lands originally belonging to the O'Hanlons who ruled southern Ulster around 1,000 years ago. The Montagu family retained the property until the 1930s. Part of their contribution to the community included providing land for the Tandragee Rovers football team, which was founded in 1909 and carried the family crest and motto, 'You may displace me but you may never change me' adopted by Sir Edward Montagu after his release from imprisonment by Queen Mary in the Tower of London during the 1500s.

Tollymore House

Tollymore House lay in the foothills of the Mourne Mountains and evolved from a shooting lodge established in the 1700s. The steep French chateau-style roofs were added in 1878 after a fire almost destroyed a world-class art collection. The collection was later sold off; among the pictures were two still lifes by Frans Snyders, part of a set of four – the other two are in the Hermitage. During the eighteenth century Viscount Limerick and his son the second Earl of Clanbrassil created a picturesque demesne from the natural woodland in association with the landscaper Thomas Wright of Durham. Unlike most landed estates Tollymore comprised mainly forestry, which was carefully managed. During the nineteenth century a sawmill operated there and oak from the estate was used for interior panelling in the *Titanic*. In 1802 Tollymore Park passed to the Countess of Roden, the Earl of Clanbrasill's sister, and remained in the family until 1955 when it was sold to the Forestry Commission. The house was demolished and the site is now a car park for visitors to Tollymore Forest Park.

Wilmont

Wilmont House lies off Belfast's Upper Malone Road, in Sir Thomas and Lady Dixon Park, and was built around 1860 by James Bristow, a director of the Northern Banking Company. The architect, Thomas Jackson, designed a double mansion for Bristow's own family and that of his son, James Thompson Bristow. It replaced a derelict house set in 180 Irish acres of land comprising forestry and a large bleach green which had belonged to the Stewarts of Ballydrain until the death of John Stewart in 1830. The Bristow family remained at Wilmont until 1866. The next owner, Robert Henry Sturrock Reade, chairman and managing director of York Street Flax Spinning Company, bought the house in 1879 (his ancestors on his mother's side had been the Stewarts of Ballydrain). He died in 1913 and his son George sold Wilmont to Sir Thomas and Lady Dixon in 1919. In 1963 Wilmont was handed over to Belfast Corporation. Lady Dixon died in 1964 and soon after the house became a home for the elderly and the grounds were opened to the public as a park, which since 1964 has hosted the Belfast International Rose Trials.

Woburn House

John Gilmore Dunbar, a Belfast mill owner, built the first Woburn House as a summer residence close to the beach south of Millisle, Co. Down, in the early nineteenth century. His nephew, George Orr Dunbar, inherited the house in 1846 and was able to extend it to its present appearance after the family's financial position improved when he married Harriet Susan Isabella Delapoer Beresford, daughter of the Archbishop of Armagh. This photograph was taken about 1910 when the house belonged to Charles W. Dunbar-Buller. It then passed to Reynell Pack-Beresford in 1924 but was sold to the Ministry of Finance after 1949 to pay for death duties incurred on his death. For a time Woburn House was a borstal but since 1981 it has been a prison officers' training school. Ghost stories emerging from the house concerning a maid and a butler who worked there have been embellished over the years – whether the ghost is actually that of the maid or the butler is unclear but the stories draw much local speculation and the house featured in a documentary on 'Northern Ireland's Greatest Haunts' in 2009 with an investigation by the Northern Ireland Paranormal Society.